Going Deeper with the

Holy Spirit

By
Benny Hinn

Going Deeper with the Holy Spirit

By Benny Hinn

Introduction

My friend, perhaps you know already how I enjoy telling people about the Holy Spirit. In these pages, I am delighted to be able to share with you even more about this wonderful third person of the Trinity and to encourage you to know and experience a relationship with Him in new and glorious ways. Join me as we discover how to experience a deeper, more intimate relationship with the blessed Holy Spirit.

Before We Begin

In the following pages, I will refer you to a number of Bible verses and Scripture passages. In some cases, you will see words that are italicized. Italics indicate that these words have been supplied or included by the translators of the King James Version. In many places, you will see words or phrases printed in boldface type. Within Bible quotations, I have used that bold type in order to emphasize a specific name or function of the Holy Spirit to help you better understand the principles we are discussing. Be blessed as you see Him revealed in God's Word!

PART I

The Person of the Holy Spirit

A s we read the Bible, we see many names that refer to
God the Father, Jesus the Son, and the Holy Spirit.
This variety of titles is not meant to cause confusion, but to
accomplish just the opposite. They are intended to help us
understand and experience the countless wonderful aspects
of the triune God. They help reveal His character and His
nature — as brilliant, as rich, and as multifaceted as a precious jewel.

God, the great "I AM" (Exodus 3:14), is referred to by
many different names throughout the Bible, each with a
specific meaning and application. For example, they range
from "Almighty God" (Genesis 17:1) to "the most High"
(Psalm 91:9) to "The Lord of hosts" and "the Holy One of
Israel" (Isaiah 54:5) to YAH or YAHWEH (Psalm 68:4).

The name of the Lord *Jesus* is the Greek form of the
Hebrew name *Joshua*, which means "YAHWEH saves". And
this is exactly what YAHWEH, the Lord God, did for us
through the shed blood of His Son, Jesus Christ.
Throughout the pages of Scripture, we also see many other
titles and names used for the Lord Jesus — from "the Prince
of Peace" (Isaiah 9:6) to "the bread of life" (John 6:48) to "the
light of the world" (John 8:12) to "the good shepherd" (John 10:11).

Likewise, the *Holy Spirit* has a variety of names
throughout Scripture. Rightly understood, these names help
us know who He really is and what He can do in our lives.

They provide tremendous insight into the will, ways, and work of the Holy Spirit. I'd like to show you what these names mean to you and how you can experience the Holy Spirit more intimately as you come to understand Him through His names.

The Holy Spirit

Perhaps the most common name you will hear for the Holy Spirit is exactly that — the **Holy Spirit**. That is not only His predominant title, but also a power-packed definition of who and what He is. He is Holy — not defiled or common, but possessing all the purity and holiness of God. He is also Spirit — not flesh, as humans are; nor having a physical body, but sharing the very invisible nature and essence of God.

Because of the incredible glory that envelopes me and floods my being when I am in the presence of the Holy Spirit, I find it difficult to put into words just how I feel when I am in His presence. Words seem inadequate and cheap when attempting to describe an experience of such incredible spiritual wealth. The dimension of His power and presence is beyond anything else I have ever experienced. The Holy Spirit can take an ordinary hotel room and transform it into a sacred cathedral by His very presence. He can take a massive arena or stadium designed for sporting events and transform it into the Holy of Holies — the place where God's presence resides and is manifest. And in the vast expanse of that arena, any individual who has been touched by the presence of the Holy Spirit can experience such dynamic fellowship and intimacy in that presence that all awareness of others fades in the light of His glory.

Indeed that is one of the functions of the Holy Spirit — to grace earthly people and places with the glorious presence of God's holiness. And when that happens, time seems to stand still.

When the Holy Spirit descends during my private devotional times or in my public ministry, I often think of Moses when he stood before the burning bush. He took off his shoes because God said, "the place whereon thou standest *is* holy ground" (Exodus 3:5). By the Holy Spirit, I am aware of the wonderful presence of God, right there in the room with me. The Holy Spirit is called *Holy* because He "is holy in Himself, quite apart from all evil."[1] He brings a sense of reverence and glory into the very atmosphere where He is.

Let's look at some of the specific places throughout Scripture where the third person of the Trinity is referred to as the Holy Spirit or the **Holy Ghost**.

- The Psalmist prayed, "Take not thy **Holy Spirit** from me" (Psalm 51:11).

- Mary became pregnant "with child of the **Holy Ghost**" (Matthew 1:18).

- The Lord Jesus declared, "If ye then, being evil, know how to give good gifts unto your children: how much more shall *your* heavenly Father give the Holy Spirit to them that ask him?" (Luke 11:13).

- Matthew said, "He shall baptize you *with* the **Holy Ghost** and with fire" (Matthew 3:11).

- The apostles wrote, "It seemed good to the **Holy Ghost**, and to us" (Acts 15:28).

- Romans 1:4 also declares Him to be **"the spirit of holiness,"** in a passage referring to the Holy Spirit's role in the resurrection of the Savior.

So we see that this name Holy Spirit carries a wealth of meaning and importance for every believer. I encourage you to get to know Him as each of these names reveals Him. Pray for a deeper understanding of His holiness and of His spiritual nature, which enables Him to be with you wherever you are, whenever you need Him.

Names That Relate the Holy Spirit to the Father

In the Bible, we see at least sixteen names for the Holy Spirit that help define His relationship with the other Persons of the Trinity—the Father and the Son. Eleven of those sixteen relate specifically to the Father. "While there is some distinction in meaning in the various titles, the chief significance is to bring out the relationship of the Holy Spirit as the third person of the Trinity, all affirming His deity and procession."[2] Let's get to know Him better by looking carefully at each of these names.

The Spirit of God

The **Spirit of God** is the name of the Holy Spirit associated with power, prophecy, and guidance.

We first encounter the Spirit of God by this name in Genesis 1—the very first chapter of the Bible. At creation, it was the Spirit of God who hovered over the face of the waters (see Genesis 1:2). Can you imagine the awesome power that was present when the universe was created? This mighty Spirit of God created all things from absolutely nothing!

Later the New Testament tells a most remarkable story about what happened when the Lord Jesus healed a demon-possessed man who was also blind and deaf. The Pharisees accused Him of using satan's power to perform such a miracle. The Lord Jesus, who knew their thoughts, declared that he "cast out devils by the **Spirit of God**" (Matthew 12:28).

- Later, the same **Spirit of God** came upon Saul and caused him to prophesy (see 1 Samuel 10:10).

- He came upon Zechariah and enabled him to proclaim the Word of the Lord (see 2 Chronicles 24:20).

- And Ezekiel's vision of the restoration of Israel was given "by the Spirit of God" (Ezekiel 11:24).

The Spirit of God is the Spirit of **prophecy**. He's the Spirit of **power**. And He is the Spirit of **guidance**. We see this as the Scripture declares in Romans 8:14: "For as many as are led by the **Spirit of God**, they are the sons of God."

Just think what it means to know that the Holy Spirit is dwelling within you—the same Holy Spirit who created the universe, the Holy Spirit who inspired prophecy, the Holy Spirit who cast out demons, and the same Spirit who raised Jesus Christ from the dead. He is living in your heart and making resurrection power available moment by moment. Hallelujah for the Spirit of God! And hallelujah that "the Spirit of God dwelleth in you" (1 Corinthians 3:16).

The Spirit of the Lord

We need to recognize that the Holy Spirit is much more than a representative of God, the Supreme Being. He is the Spirit of the Yahweh we worship, the Spirit of the "I AM," the Spirit of the Lord of heaven and earth. This title for the Holy Spirit, the **Spirit of the Lord**, is used repeatedly in both the Old and New Testaments.

I love the story of Gideon. After years of oppression by the Midianites, Gideon answered God's call on behalf of the Israelites. Scripture tells us that "The Spirit of the Lord came upon Gideon," and he called his armies together (Judges 6:34). Thirty-two thousand men came to fight. The Lord told Gideon that there were too many men in the army. He did not want Israel to be able to brag about winning the battle because of their large number. He wanted them to be convinced that He alone had made them triumph and given them the victory.

So He asked Gideon to reduce the army to 300 men whose only weapons were a lamp and a trumpet. When these soldiers surrounded the vast armies of Midian and blew their trumpets, the enemy fled. It was the Spirit of the Lord who led Gideon to such a glorious triumph.

- Isaiah said, "When the enemy shall come in like a flood, the **Spirit of the Lord** shall lift up a standard against him" (Isaiah 59:19).

- When the Lord Jesus began His ministry, He stood in the synagogue and quoted Isaiah saying, "The **Spirit of the Lord** is upon Me..." (Luke 4:18).

- Paul used the same title to explain the workings of the mighty, victorious Spirit of the Lord, who uses His power to free us: "Now the Lord is that Spirit" and where the **Spirit of the Lord** *is*, there *is* liberty" (2 Corinthians 3:17).

My Spirit

When God speaks of the Holy Spirit, He does it in a very personal way. He refers to Him as "**My Spirit**," clearly demonstrating the mystery of the Trinity and affirming that the Holy Spirit is a vital part of the Godhead. The Father, the Son, and the Holy Spirit are one God, yet they are three distinct personalities.

- God declared through Joel that in the last days before Christ's return, "I will pour out **my spirit** upon all flesh" (Joel 2:28).

- He also warned people everywhere in Genesis 6:3 to heed the Holy Spirit, saying, "**My spirit** shall not always strive with man."

- Zechariah reminded us that it is not by might or power, but "by **my spirit**, saith the Lord of hosts" (Zechariah 4:6).

The Spirit of the Living God

I love the work of the Holy Spirit. He makes God's Word so real *to* us and *in* us. The Scriptures associate the name **Spirit of the Living God** with the work of the Holy Spirit in making His Word come alive and in making His children "living epistles" (see 2 Corinthians 3:2-3). When we become living epistles, we are like a letter written to tell everyone about the goodness of God.

Instead of concentrating their efforts on being "living epistles" and giving the glory to the Lord, it is unfortunately true that sometimes some ministers may try to establish their importance by talking about the number of people in their church, the square footage of their buildings, the size of their mailing list, the number and size of their crusades, how many potential viewers exist for their broadcasts, how large their budget is, etc. But for me there is only one test, and it's very simple: Are lives changed? And how are lives changed? By the Spirit of the Living God.

Ledger sheets and membership rolls may be necessary for administration, but they are not important from an eternal perspective. People are important. And all that matters is that people are set free and able to enjoy abundant life by the Spirit of the living God. A person who is miraculously transformed by the Spirit of the living God is a living epistle — a walking, breathing testimonial of the power of the living God in the world today. Dear saint of God, I pray that you will go deeper with the Holy Spirit and begin to enjoy the highest level of liberation and abundance possible by the Holy Spirit. If you are not, all you need to do is ask. He is also your Helper and He will set you in places of freedom and plenty that you have only dreamed of before.

Paul was so clear on this when some of the people at the church of Corinth questioned his credentials. His reply was simple: all of the people in the church at Corinth were his credentials *because of the Spirit of the living God.* Read what he wrote:

"Do we begin again to commend ourselves? or need we, as some *others*, epistles of commendation to you, or *letters* of commendation from you? Ye are our epistle written in our hearts, known and read of all men: *Forasmuch as ye* are manifestly declared to be the epistle of Christ ministered by us, written not with ink, but with the **Spirit of the living God**; not in the tables of stone, but in fleshly tables of the heart. And such trust have we through Christ to God-ward: Not that we are sufficient of ourselves to think any thing as of ourselves; but our sufficiency *is* of God; Who also hath made us able ministers of the new testament; not of the letter, but of the spirit: for the letter killeth, but the spirit giveth life."

2 Corinthians 3:1-6

I believe you are longing, as I am, for a fresh anointing of the Spirit that will change your life and impact others through your walk with the Lord. Let us pray that we will be consumed by our longing to be used of God and to know His presence in a greater dimension than ever before.

The Power of the Highest

When I get to heaven, there are many people and heroes of the faith whom I want to meet. Mary, the mother of Jesus, is one of those individuals. In all of history, she alone encountered **"the power of the Highest"** in a way that has never been experienced before or since.

I want to know what it was like to experience God's power in the way Mary did. Oh, how I wish even now to sit with the great prophets of the Old Testament and discover things I am so hungry for. How I wish I could sit with Peter and ask him about the experience he had when his very shadow healed the sick; or with Paul who, when God's presence descended so strongly upon him, he was caught up to the third heaven. But Mary's experience with the Holy Spirit stands out as one of the greatest in Scripture.

As you know, one of the great central teachings and prophecies of Scripture is that the Messiah would be born of a virgin: "Therefore the Lord himself shall give you a sign; Behold, a virgin shall conceive, and bear a son, and shall call his name Immanuel" (Isaiah 7:14).

When Mary learned from the angel Gabriel that she would bear the Messiah, she asked the natural question: "How shall this be, seeing I know not a man?" (Luke 1:34).

Scripture records Gabriel's powerful reply, "The Holy Ghost shall come upon thee, and the **power of the Highest** shall overshadow thee: therefore also that holy thing which shall be born of thee shall be called the Son of God" (Luke 1:35).

Of course, that's exactly what happened. The impossible becomes possible when "the power of the Highest" comes.

Have you heard the story about the little boy who was trying to move a huge rock? He pulled and pushed, straining with all his might against this great rock. He even tried to move it with leverage from a board, but the rock would not budge.

His dad asked him, "Son, have you used all your resources?"

The son answered, "Yes, Dad. I've tried everything and I can't make it move."

His father replied, "No, you haven't. You haven't asked me to help you yet."

I know that, like I am, you are hungry to see God's power transform your life, your relationships, and your work. Surrender anew to the Holy Spirit and invite the full measure of the power of the Highest to be unleashed in your life!

Names That Relate the Holy Spirit to Jesus Christ the Son

We know that Jesus Christ is the Son of God. We know that, together, the Father, the Son, and the Holy Spirit comprise the Godhead, or the Trinity. As I explained the names of the Holy Spirit, I want to help you understand this wonderful mystery of the triune God. Now that you have read about the Holy Spirit's relationship to God the Father, let's look at the way He relates to Jesus the Son.

The Spirit of Christ

I once took a ski trip to the breathtaking Rocky Mountains in Colorado. The best part of the whole experience was the lift ride to the top—the beautiful snow-covered slopes below looked so peaceful and inviting. They gave no indication of the misery in store for an inexperienced skier (like I was) who actually tried to ski down from the summit. As the lift carried us higher and higher, I realized that what looked like a single mountain was actually a series of peaks, separated by valleys. Looking at the mountains from the ground, I could not tell where one started and another ended. Only when I got closer to the peaks did this become clear.

Similarly, long before the Lord Jesus Christ came to live on earth, the prophets foretold the majestic mountaintop experience of salvation He would bring. They saw the two great peaks of Bible prophecy. They believed Christ would come to earth as the *suffering* Messiah, and also as the *conquering* Messiah. Yet from their perspective, the events foretold regarding the coming Messiah appeared as one mountaintop to the prophets of old. Although they saw His two great missions — suffering for the sins of mankind and conquering this fallen world — I'm sure they did not always understand the full significance and meaning of the words they spoke and were unclear as to when these events would actually occur.

I think this is what Peter wrote about when he declared, "Of which salvation the prophets have enquired and searched diligently, who prophesied of the grace *that should come* unto you: Searching what, or what manner of time **the Spirit of Christ** which was in them did signify, when it testified beforehand of the sufferings of Christ, and the glory that should follow" (1 Peter 1:10-11). The title, **the Spirit of Christ**, is so interesting here in this prophetic passage because it is a reminder of several things. I want to emphasize two of them.

First, it reminds us that the Spirit of the Lord inspired the human authors of Scripture: "For prophecy came not in old time by the will of man: but holy men of God spake *as they were* moved by the Holy Ghost" (2 Peter 1:21). Related to this is the clear testimony of the Word that the work of the Holy Spirit is to lift up the Lord Jesus Christ. The Lord Jesus said, "He shall testify of me" (John 15:26).

Second, it reminds us that the Scriptures focus on Jesus Christ. "The testimony of Jesus is the spirit of prophecy" (Revelation 19:10). Prophecy is all about the Lord Jesus, so when the Spirit of the Lord is involved with prophecies and prophets, He is working to proclaim the message of the Lord Jesus.

The Spirit of Jesus Christ

Philippians is such a marvelous book! Written from a dark, damp Roman prison cell, Paul teaches us in this book how we can have joy in spite of the *place* we're in, the *people* we're with, or the *person* we are. That's pretty remarkable when you think about it. Just about every challenge we face comes from one of these areas. How could Paul be so confident of joyful living in the midst of challenging circumstances? After all, he was in prison, shackled to a Roman soldier twenty-four hours a day. And in the midst of this, his reputation was being attacked by fellow believers. He himself gives us the answer: "For I know that this shall turn to my salvation through your prayer, and the supply of the **Spirit of Jesus Christ**" (Philippians 1:19).

Part of the great comforting work of the Holy Spirit is to give us peace and even joy in situations like these. In the context of this book about joy, it makes sense that Paul would identify the connecting link to joy as the **Spirit of Jesus Christ**. After all, the Lord Jesus wanted our joy to be full and complete (see John 16:24) and, just before He was crucified, He prayed for the Father to send *another* Helper to abide with us and make our joy complete. The Holy Spirit that Jesus prayed for is the One who truly does bring the joy that the Savior wanted each of us to have.

So you see, joy comes through the Spirit of Jesus Christ regardless of our circumstances. The joy that you want, the joy that you are so diligently searching for, the joy that your spirit is crying out for only truly comes from one Person: the Spirit of Jesus Christ.

The Spirit of His Son

"And because ye are sons, God hath sent forth the **Spirit of his Son** into your hearts, crying, Abba, Father. Wherefore thou art no more a servant, but a son; and if a son, then an heir of God through Christ" (Galatians 4:6-7).

If you've read any of my previous books or been present in any of my services, you've probably heard me talk about my earthly father. The best way I can describe the way our father ran our family is to ask you to remember the father in the movie, *The Sound of Music.* Except for the location and the singing, our house functioned much like the Von Trapp household did—strict discipline, well-understood instructions, comprehensive rules, everything neat and tidy, and plenty of work to do. When we failed to live up to the standards set for us, swift punishment was sure. Our home was run with military-like discipline. My brothers and sisters and I were even dressed in matching uniforms.

A former boxer, my father was a 6'2", 260-pound powerhouse. But even that doesn't begin to describe him. By virtue of his commanding personality, he really was larger than life. And there was never any doubt that he was in charge.

In his own way, he loved us. And I never doubted his love for any of us, even though I don't remember hearing him express it audibly very often until the very end of his life. For nearly the first thirty years of my life, my father's stern ways, combined with his type of personality, presented him as detached, distant, and somewhat cold emotionally. I don't think he was intentionally that way, but by his very makeup he was undemonstrative. And my speech impediment didn't make communicating with him any easier. Although I was his first-born son and I grew up under the same roof, ate bread from his table, and enjoyed the physical provision he made for our family, I never really knew what it was to have a close relationship with him until I was an adult. It wasn't until he was born again that I experienced the relationship that I had always longed for.

Knowing that, can you imagine the joy I experienced when I met the Lord and instantly felt a tremendous intimacy and affection with my heavenly Father? What took me thirty years to experience with my earthly father took me less than thirty seconds to experience with my heavenly Father.

I will never, ever lose my appreciation for the relationship the Holy Spirit gives me with the Father because of the sacrifice of the Lord Jesus. I'm no longer a slave to sin and alienated from the Father. I'm not in the Father's family as a stepchild—emotionally distant and never really accepted. I've been adopted as a full-fledged son and joint-heir, and so I can cry out, "Abba, Father!" (see Galatians 4:6). All of these benefits are yours, too, through the precious Holy Spirit.

I want you to understand that "Abba" is an Aramaic term that small children would use in addressing their father, like "Daddy" or "Papa." The term is polite and intimate, even tender. And how can it be that we can have this kind of relationship with the Father? "God hath sent forth **the Spirit of his Son** into (our) hearts, crying 'Abba, Father'" (Galatians 4:6). Oh, my friend, come to know the Lord as your Abba today.

Names That Relate to the Holy Spirit's Work in Our Lives

You have seen how the Holy Spirit works in relation to the Father and to the Son. Now, I hope you have a better understanding of the way the Trinity functions. But there is one more important relationship that the Holy Spirit enjoys—His relationship with you!

The Spirit of Adoption

Something wonderful happens the moment we believe on Jesus Christ as our Savior. We are adopted into God's family. Instantly, we are given power to become children of God (see John 1:12). It is a fulfillment of the Father's great plan. He called us to "adoption of children by Jesus Christ to himself, according to the good pleasure of his will" (Ephesians 1:5).

Who arranges for our adoption? The Holy Spirit. Paul writes, "For as many as are led by the Spirit of God, they are the sons of God. For ye have not received the spirit of bondage again to fear; but ye have received the **Spirit of adoption**" (Romans 8:14-15).

The concept of adoption points to two great truths, both conveyed by the Holy Spirit. The first one is mentioned above. It is the great *fact* of our adoption into God's family with all the rights, privileges, and responsibilities that are a part of being a member of the family.

The second one is the great *fulfillment* of adoption—the transformation of our bodies at the Rapture when we *receive* the promised inheritance: "And not only they, but ourselves also, which have the firstfruits of the Spirit, even we ourselves groan within ourselves, **waiting for the adoption**, *to wit*, the redemption of our body" (Romans 8:23).

The most wonderful miracle we have ever seen won't compare to that great miracle of the Rapture when we'll exchange our mortal bodies for immortal bodies—bodies that will never be subject to sickness, disease, or death. Don't get me wrong, until that day everyone should absolutely seek their miracle from the Lord. You may be wondering, *what is the foretaste or firstfruits of this great miracle to come?* The Spirit of Adoption! When will our adoption be culminated? When our bodies are redeemed at the Rapture. What a glorious day! Come quickly, Lord Jesus!

The Spirit of Glory

It seems more and more evident to me that Christians are coming under attack— especially in North America. I also see these attacks increasing in intensity. That's why I believe in what I call "violent faith"—faith that isn't passive, that doesn't tiptoe around, that isn't afraid of what people think, or that does not fear the consequences of being aggressive.

Peter wrote his first epistle to believers in Asia Minor who were experiencing the sting of persecution. He strongly and boldly declared, "If ye be reproached for the name of

Christ, happy *are ye*; for **the spirit of glory and of God** resteth upon you" (1 Peter 4:14).

The Holy Spirit, speaking through Peter, gave these courageous believers two great assurances as they endured persecution. First, He assured them that they hadn't done anything wrong or believed anything wrong. Instead, their persecution showed that the very Spirit of the Lord rested upon them. Second, He promised these brave believers that His glory would rest on them. He was talking about the magnificent glory of God—the same glory that the nation of Israel experienced in the wilderness and appeared as a cloud by day and the pillar of fire by night; the same glory that the high priest experienced in the Holy of Holies; the same glory that appeared to the shepherds keeping watch the night the Lord Jesus was born; the same glory that came upon the Apostles in the Upper Room. This is the same glory that will be ours forever when we allow that glory to strengthen us.

Now believe me, I'm no stranger to persecution. When I trusted Christ, my whole family turned against me and ostracized me. But as I held firm, the Holy Spirit came upon me with His glory, energizing my spirit and giving me the strength to go on. Soon my entire family came to know Christ as Savior. For each of you who feels he is standing alone in the midst of opposition, take heart—the Holy Spirit of glory has promised to rest on *you* and He *will* keep His promise!

The Spirit of Grace

Have you taken time lately to reflect on the wonder of salvation? Without salvation, we would still be "without Christ, being aliens from the commonwealth of Israel, and strangers from the covenants of promise, **having no hope, and without God in the world**" (Ephesians 2:12). It is God's grace, His kindness and undeserved favor, that reached out to us. Even when we were His enemies He saved us. His amazing grace covered our guilt with His righteousness. His grace keeps us, for we were *saved by grace* through faith and *kept by grace* through faith. His grace brings us to the foot of the cross, unable to brag, able simply to say that our best was as filthy rags in His sight. His grace that not only covers our failures—it transforms them into distinctive points of power and ministry.[4]

Because of His grace, He gifts us and enables us to experience the joy of service, and the delight of laboring with the Savior as He builds His Church. Because of His grace, He puts resurrection power at our disposal, allowing us to persevere and prevail. Because of His grace, He rewards us, even in our unworthiness. Because of His grace, He indwells us, allowing us to experience the richness of moment-by-moment fellowship with the Spirit of the Lord. Because of His grace, He is returning for us, to transform us and allow us to experience the wonder of all He has prepared for us.

As Paul reflected on God's grace in salvation, he couldn't help but break out in a hymn of praise for God's grace in executing His plan of redemption: "O the depth of the riches both of the wisdom and knowledge of God! how unsearchable *are* his judgments, and his ways past finding out! For who hath known the mind of the Lord? or who has been his counselor? Or who hath first given to him, and it shall be recompensed unto him again? For of him, and through him, and to him, *are* all things: to whom *be* glory for ever. Amen" (Romans 11:33-36).

How marvelous is the grace of God! And who do you suppose conveys this grace to us? The Holy Spirit. He is the very Spirit of grace and He ministers the Lord's grace to us moment by moment.

Yet, incredibly, some people feel the temptation to abandon the cause of Christ, to forsake the streams of living water for dry, empty creekbeds. The Book of Hebrews was written, in part, to convince these people not to forsake the Lord. The Scripture declares: "He that despised Moses' law died without mercy under two or three witnesses: Of how much sorer punishment, suppose ye, shall he be thought worthy, who hath trodden under foot the Son of God, and hath counted the blood of the covenant, wherewith he was sanctified, an unholy thing, and hath done despite unto the Spirit of grace?" (Hebrews 10:28-29).

Rejecting God's Law brought swift and thorough judgment in Old Testament days. How much more, then, should we fear the consequences of holding in contempt the Son of God, His sacrifice, the Spirit of God, and His grace? The Father will not take lightly the despising of the Son and the Spirit. He warns us plainly in His Word: "*It is* a fearful thing to fall into the hands of the living God" (Hebrews 10:31).

The Spirit of Grace and of Supplication

There are some people who minimize the importance of Bible prophecy, and even some who make fun of it. Mark Twain said, "If the world comes to an end, I want to be in Cincinnati — things always come twenty years later in Cincinnati." But it's important to realize that 25 percent of the Bible is prophetic in nature — an amount equal in size to the entire New Testament. Do you think God would devote 25 percent of His Word to an *unimportant* subject? I certainly do not.

I am waiting and watching for the Rapture, the inauguration of so many of the great prophetic events of Scripture. Martin Luther, the father of the Protestant Reformation, said he only had *two* days on his calendar — today and "that day!"[5] That's the way I want to be, too! I want to live today for "that day!"

One of the great prophetic passages of Scripture is Zechariah 12. It describes the reconciliation of the Jewish people with the Savior they rejected. This great event occurs at the Second Coming of Christ. Try to imagine the profound emotion of this moment.

On the one hand is the Lord Jesus, the rejected King, now returned as Conqueror. The One who said with such emotion, "O Jerusalem, Jerusalem, *thou* that killest the prophets, and stonest them which are sent unto thee, how often would I have gathered thy children together, even as a hen gathereth her chickens under *her* wings, **and** ye would not!" (Matthew 23:37).

On the other hand is the Jewish nation. They have lived through the horrors of the Tribulation. They have seen the awesome power of the glorified Savior returning to earth with His armies to destroy His enemies. And now in a moment of time they realize that the One they had so steadfastly rejected is the precious Son of God and they turn to Him in faith. Who prepared the way for this reconciliation? The Holy Spirit!

More than five hundred years before Christ, the Lord described this scene to the prophet Zechariah: "And I will pour upon the house of David, and on the inhabitants of Jerusalem, the spirit of **grace and of supplications:** and [or "so that" in the NASB] they shall look upon me whom they have pierced, and they shall mourn for him, as one mourneth for *his* only *son*, and it shall be in bitterness for him, as one that is in bitterness for *his* firstborn" (Zechariah 12:10).

When the Lord poured out His Spirit upon His battered and bedraggled people, He broke through their resistance so they could experience God's *favor* (grace), and that freed their hearts to call out to Him in *repentance*.

"Supplication" as it is used here to describe the Holy Spirit refers "less [to a] formal entreaty . . . than the outpourings of a troubled soul."[6] That's what the Holy Spirit does. No matter what we've done or how we have failed, He helps us come to the Father in freedom and find the forgiveness and mercy so abundantly available to all.

The Spirit of Wisdom and Understanding

Isaiah 11 is one of those mountaintop passages of Scripture — so powerful and moving. As Isaiah describes the coming of the Messiah in verse 2 of this great chapter, he uses a series of three couplets to describe the work of the Holy Spirit in the life and ministry of Christ Jesus:

The spirit of wisdom and understanding
The spirit of counsel and might
The spirit of knowledge and of the fear of the Lord

As part of the Godhead, one of the attributes of the Holy Spirit is that He is unchanging. You can always, always count on Him because He stays the same. Because of His constancy, we can expect that the Holy Spirit will make manifest these same qualities in *us as* we allow Him to work.

The first couplet describes Him as "the spirit of wisdom and understanding" (Isaiah 11:2).

Wisdom is nothing more than living with skill. It goes beyond intellectual knowledge to include the ability to apply the knowledge of God's Word in our daily life — and nothing less. It involves using knowledge in the right way to select the right ends. Then wisdom directs us to achieve those ends in a proper fashion. It involves applying God's truth to human experience. Properly mastered, it can lead to a happy and successful life.

This skillful living manifested itself in the life of the
Lord Jesus even from His childhood. As a child, Jesus was
"filled with wisdom" and "increased in wisdom" (Luke 2:40, 52).

Wisdom was also evident in His preaching: "And when
the Sabbath day was come, he began to teach in the synagogue: and many hearing *him* were astonished, saying,
'From whence hath this *man* these things? and what wisdom is this which is given unto him, that such mighty works
are wrought by his hands'" (Mark 6:2). They marveled at
the wisdom of His words, and at the practical skill His
words imparted. And did you notice the connection they
made between the wisdom of His teaching and His mighty
works: "wisdom . . . that such mighty works are wrought by
his hands!" Wisdom is about actions as well as words.

And because godly wisdom is so rare, the wisdom of
Jesus' actions routinely baffled and angered those without
this wisdom. The Lord Jesus recounted the words of His
critics: "The Son of man came eating and drinking, and they
say, Behold a man gluttonous, and a winebibber, a friend of
publicans and sinners. But wisdom is justified of her children" (Matthew 11:19). And the mighty, Spirit-led growth of
the Church, growing in every continent and country, every
village and community and country bears ample testimony
to the wisdom of the Master's strategy. "But wisdom is justified of all her children" (Luke 7:35). In other words, wisdom is proven by the right actions of those who practice it.

Understanding is the same as having discernment in
wisdom. It is not about the accumulation of facts. The idea
here is that a person with "understanding" has the insight

to choose with skill between the options that come his way. "*Bin* [the Hebrew word for "understanding" in Isaiah 11] is the power of judgment and perspective insight and is demonstrated in the use of knowledge."[7]

This kind of perception comes from the Holy Spirit, but not automatically. We must diligently seek it. Proverbs, known as the book of wisdom, puts it this way in chapter 2, verses 1 through 6: "My son, if thou wilt receive my words, and hide my commandments with thee; So that thou incline thine ear unto wisdom, *and* apply thine heart to understanding; Yea, if thou criest after knowledge, *and* liftest up thy voice for understanding; If thou seekest her as silver, and searchest for her as *for* hid treasures; Then shalt thou understand the fear of the Lord, and find the knowledge of God. For the Lord giveth wisdom: out of his mouth *cometh* knowledge and understanding."

Since this understanding comes from God alone, the wicked are infamous for their lack of ability to perceive the wisdom of the Lord: "The righteous considereth the cause of the poor: *but* the wicked regardeth not to know *it*" (Proverbs 29:7).

What an incredible comfort these words are for the righteous! There are many choices, alternatives, and options in the world. Sometimes it seems impossible to choose between them. Thanks be to God that, through the Holy Spirit, we can have *wisdom* (skill in living life), and *understanding* (discernment to choose between the alternatives we face).

With the counsel and might of the Holy Spirit in our hearts and minds, our perspective is fresh and full of insight, and our outlook is optimistic. But without it, this present existence is at best dark, dreary, and depressing. Bertrand Russell, one of the foremost atheists of our time, described his perspective on life this way: "The life of man is a long march through night surrounded by invisible foes, tortured by weariness and pain, toward a goal that few can hope to reach and where none can tarry long. One by one as they march, our comrades vanish from our sight, seized by the silent orders of omnipotent death. Brief and powerless is man's life. On him and all his race the slow sure doom falls, pitiless and dark. Blind to good and evil, reckless of destruction, omnipotent matter rolls on its relentless way. For man, condemned today to lose his dearest, tomorrow himself to pass through the gates of darkness, it remains only to cherish, ere the blow falls, the lofty thoughts that ennoble his little day."[8]

The Spirit of Counsel and Might

In the second of three couplets, Isaiah describes the Holy Spirit as **"the spirit of counsel and might"** (Isaiah 11:2).

I'm so glad the Holy Spirit as our Counselor gives us the meaning and fulfillment in life which Bertrand Russell so desperately needed. But there is no doubt that his is the way the ungodly view life. It is bankrupt and utterly meaningless for them.

As the prophet Isaiah emphasized, the Holy Spirit was "the spirit of counsel and might". In Isaiah 11:2, he is prophesying again about the coming of the Lord Jesus. It is the counsel and might of the Holy Spirit in the mystery of the Trinity that allow the Lord Jesus to be called "Wonderful, Counsellor" and "The mighty God" (Isaiah 9:6). "The attributes of the Holy Spirit would characterize the Messiah. Because of His wisdom, understanding, counsel, and knowledge He is the Wonderful Counsellor" (see Isaiah 9:6).[9]

The Holy Spirit also delights to counsel us. He is not only able, but He really wants to help you. Quit trying to figure it out all by yourself; and let the Holy Spirit counsel you! Stop trying to muster the power to push your way through things. With the Holy Spirit, your motto can be, "Not somehow, but *triumphantly!*"

One of my friends told me the story of his great-grandparents. They went from a barely-scraping-by existence in Kentucky to Oklahoma because they heard that it was the land of opportunity. The land they farmed wasn't very productive and consequently they never had much to live on. They scraped out an existence just as they had before. Eventually they sold the land and moved to another state.

The person who bought the land from them discovered oil and became wealthy. The reason the land didn't farm well was that it was so saturated with petroleum that nothing would grow. Think of it! For years these dear people lived near poverty when at their very feet was all they needed—not only to survive, but to thrive! If they had dug a little deeper, rich oil would have erupted and they could have enjoyed the reality of financial success and peace of mind!

In the same way we have the great resources of the Holy Spirit at our disposal, and yet some of us live our lives in spiritual poverty and frustration, not using the riches that are at our *immediate* beck and call. We simply need to go deeper. Not only does He give us guidance, but He imparts the strength and energy to carry out His plans. Remember, the Lord Jesus said, "But ye shall receive power, after that the Holy Ghost is come upon you" (Acts 1:8).

The Spirit of Knowledge and of the Fear of the Lord

The third couplet in Isaiah 11:2 describes the Holy Spirit as **"the spirit of knowledge and of the fear of the Lord."** He not only *is* that Spirit, He imparts "knowledge and the fear of the Lord" to us.

The word *knowledge* here refers to the knowledge we gain through our senses, both about how the world works and about God's moral law. Thus, the Holy Spirit gives us the ability to look at the world and perceive His handiwork and purposes in it. The Bible declares that "the invisible things of him from the creation of the world are clearly seen, being understood by the things that are made, *even* His eternal power and Godhead" (Romans 1:20). When we are in tune with the leading of the Holy Spirit, we gain a fuller understanding of the world around us, and every day can be packed with awe and wonder.

But not only does He bring knowledge, the Holy Spirit also brings "the fear of the Lord." This is so important to understand. Solomon, under the inspiration of the Holy Spirit, said, "The fear of the Lord *is* the beginning of knowledge: *but* fools despise wisdom and instruction" (Proverbs 1:7).

Now I don't want you to misunderstand my next thoughts. I'm grateful for all the emphasis these days on spiritual warfare. I believe it has made us more sensitive to the spiritual struggles going on around us. But I fear that an unintended result of all this teaching is that men and women now fear the devil more than they fear God. I tell you, *"Fear God, and you will not need to fear the devil."* You'll be aware of his power and act accordingly as the archangel Michael did (see Jude 8, 9), but you will not fear the devil for "greater is he that is in you, than he that is in the world" (1 John 4:4).

By the way, there is a difference between fearing the Lord and being afraid. Exodus 19 and 20 show this so beautifully. The nation of Israel is gathered at Mt. Sinai to enter into a covenant relationship with YAHWEH and receive the Ten Commandments from Him. Mt. Sinai was ablaze with "thunders and lightnings, and a thick cloud [was] upon the mount, and the voice of the trumpet exceeding loud; so that all the people that *was* in the camp trembled" (Exodus 19:16).

In fact, the nation of Israel said to Moses, "Speak thou with us, and we will hear: but let not God speak with us, lest we die" (Exodus 20:19).

Then Moses utters these remarkable words: "**Fear not:** for God is come to prove you, **and that his fear may be before your faces**, that ye sin not" (Exodus 20:20). He was saying, "Don't be *afraid*, but *fear!*" See the difference? The people were trembling at God's power. But what the Father wanted was for them to have a healthy respect of His power that would lead to a sense of awe which would then keep them from sinning. The "fear of the Lord" doesn't mean being *afraid*, it means *understanding* Him and *respecting* Him such that we live a life of loving obedience.

And who brings this ability to fear the Lord? The Holy Spirit!

The Spirit of Life

I love the words of the Lord Jesus, "I have come that they might have life, and that they might have *it* more abundantly" (John 10:10). Abundant life—there is some-thing so compelling about that, something that says within us, "Yes, I *must* have this." And who ministers this abun-dant life to us? The Holy Spirit. The Lord Jesus said, "It is the spirit that quickeneth; the flesh profiteth nothing: the words that I speak unto you, *they* are spirit, and *they* are life" (John 6:63). Now the life He's talking about is salva-tion, but it is also true that "what God promises for eternity, he begins to do in this lifetime."[10]

Oh my dear friend, when the Spirit of the Lord comes, He brings *life*—breaking the power of canceled sin and death. Whatever has died in you can live again just by His touch! And He brings not just endless life, but *better* life *right now*. Paul says, "The law of the **Spirit of life** in Christ Jesus hath made me free from the law of sin and death" (Romans 8:2).

Are you experiencing all the life the Holy Spirit has for you? Someone gave me this quote, and I think it sums up the issue magnificently: "I believe that only one person in a thousand knows the trick of really living in the present. Most of us spend fifty-eight minutes each hour either living in the past, regretting for lost joys, or feeling shame for things badly done (both utterly useless and weakening); or living the future which we either long for or dread. The only way to live is to accept each minute as an unrepeatable miracle, which is exactly what it is — a miracle that will not be repeated."[11] The Spirit of the Lord is waiting just now to *heal* your past, *guarantee* your future, and *liberate* you to experience abundant life right now.

The Holy Spirit of Promise

Paul declared that those who trusted Christ as their Savior are "sealed with the Holy Spirit of promise, which is the earnest of our inheritance" (Ephesians 1:13-14). I want you to notice two things.

First, He is the **"Holy Spirit of promise."** That is, "the promised Spirit."[12] The Lord Jesus *promised* in the Upper Room Discourse that He would send the Holy Spirit, but the Lord Jesus made the promise *in conjunction with* the Father. He is called the Holy Spirit, the One, "whom the Father will send in my name" (John 14:26). He also said, "I will send unto you from the Father, . . . which proceedeth from the Father" (John 15:26). Thus the Holy Spirit was promised by the Father as well, and is termed in Acts 1:4, "the promise of the Father." Because of their faith in the words of the Father and the Son, that early band in Jerusalem took God at His word and waited for the Holy Spirit. And God did not disappoint them.

Don't ever forget that "God *is* not a man, that He should lie; neither the son of man, that he should repent: hath he said, and shall he not do *it*? or hath he spoken, and shall he not make it good?" (Numbers 23:19). Some people would have you believe that God's Word, the Bible, isn't true, or isn't completely true. Regardless of how they articulate their words, what they're doing is calling each member of the godhead a liar. It's an old saying but a true one: "God said it. I believe it. That settles it." And might I add, "I'm going to live like it." Just like the expectant followers in the Upper Room, take Him at His word in *everything* He says.

Second, the indwelling of the Holy Spirit is a promise that one day we will receive all that has been promised and prepared for us: a *new* body, a *new* nature, and a *new* home. The Holy Spirit living within us is demonstrating, moment by moment, that God will one day present us with the full measure of our inheritance. That will be a wonderful day!

The Spirit of Truth

Another one of the great titles ascribed to the promise of the Father is the **Spirit of truth**. The Holy Spirit has a specific assignment from God to communicate and impart what is true and valid. The Lord Jesus described Him as "the Spirit of truth; whom the world cannot receive, because it seeth him not, neither knoweth him: but ye know him; for he dwelleth with you, and shall be in you" (John 14:17).

Not only does He teach truth, He *is* truth.

He will teach you the truth about *Jesus* (the direct meaning of John 14:17).[13]

He will teach you the truth about the *Bible*. The Lord Jesus declared, "When he, the Spirit of truth, is come, he will guide you into all truth" (John 16:13; see also 1 Corinthians 2:10-11).

He will teach you the truth about *yourself*. David was so refreshingly honest when he asked the Lord, "Who can understand his errors? cleanse thou me from secret *faults*" (Psalm 19:12). No one can fully discern his or her own errors, but as we listen to the voice of the Holy Spirit and follow His prompting, areas in our lives that are invisible to us will be refined and sublimated by the Holy Spirit. "But we all, with open face beholding as in a glass the glory of the Lord, are changed into the same image from glory to glory, *even* as by the Spirit of the Lord" (2 Corinthians 3:18).

The Comforter

If you have ever had to appear to defend yourself in court or before the government, you know what a harrowing experience it can be. Although our American justice system dictates that a person is innocent until proven guilty, that's rarely how an individual in that situation actually *feels*. What you feel is powerless, alone, and hurting. Oh, how you long for someone to help you bear the burden.

I have good news! In a spiritual sense, this is exactly what the Holy Spirit does. The Lord said, "I will pray the Father, and he shall give you another Comforter, that he may abide with you for ever" (John 14:16). Jesus, in this verse is promising another Comforter. The word *comforter* in the Greek language is *paraclete* — meaning, "one called alongside to help." In natural terms, a paraclete is like a defense attorney, an advocate, a helper who will fight your battles. In spiritual terms, the Holy Spirit does all this and more. He is a Helper who is so good at what He does that He calms your restless fears and stills your troubled heart.

Mere words are totally insufficient to express the depth of my love toward the Holy Spirit for the many ways and the many times He has helped me. He truly has been my constant Helper and Comforter. And when I stand before the people to preach the gospel, He is there beside me, helping me. As Paul said, "My speech and my preaching *was* not with enticing words of man's wisdom, but in demonstration of the Spirit and of power (1 Corinthians 2:4).

Praise God for our Comforter!

The Eternal Spirit

As a Member of the Godhead, the Holy Spirit was present before time, has been present in every moment in history, and will remain after, as the old hymn says, "time shall be no more."

The writer of the Book of Hebrews recognized the Holy Spirit's eternal nature when he wrote that if the blood of bulls and goats was once used as a sacrifice, "How much more shall the blood of Christ, who through the **eternal Spirit** offered himself without spot to God, purge your conscience from dead works to serve the living God?" (Hebrews 9:14).

Just as the Melchizedekian priesthood of Christ is superior to the priesthood of the Old Testament, so the redemption effected through the eternal Spirit is superior to the temporary remedies of the law — remedies designed not so much to redeem man as to point out man's *need* for redemption through faith in Christ.

Saying that He is an "eternal" Spirit is the same as saying He is a "divine" Spirit. His existence is infinite. "The term *eternal*, which with all propriety can also be assigned to God the Father or God the Son, is here assigned to the Holy Spirit. Since to God alone this attribute may be predicated, the Spirit is understood as God."[14]

The Spirit

The Word of God gives many wonderful names to the Holy Spirit, but perhaps the most unadorned name is the most profound. He is often referred to in the Scriptures simply as "**the Spirit**."

That was the term John the Baptist used when he described what happened at the baptism of the Lord Jesus. He said, "I saw **the Spirit** descending from heaven like a dove, and it abode upon him." (John 1:32). You might even say, *the* Spirit, the unique Spirit, the *one and only* Spirit, for after all, in person, in work, and in our personal experience of His indwelling, there is none like Him.

The Lord Jesus also used the same words. He declared to Nicodemus, "Except a man be born *of* water and of **the Spirit**, he cannot enter into the kingdom of God" (John 3:5).

Again and again, we are encouraged to "be filled with *the Spirit*" (Ephesians 5:18; see Acts 9:17).

The names given to the Holy Spirit are significant and glorious. But they are not given simply that we may know *about* Him. They are names we can use every day to truly know Him and welcome Him into the very recesses of our lives.

Yes, He is the Spirit of the Father and the Son. But He is ready to be your Paraclete—your Counselor, your Helper, your Teacher and your Guide. He is here to be the Spirit of glory and grace, the Spirit of wisdom and knowledge and might, the very Spirit of the living God and of Jesus Christ in your life today.

PART II
The Work of the Holy Spirit

N ow that you understand the Holy Spirit better because of His names, I want you to understand Him better because of His work. One of the greatest things the Holy Spirit does is to change people. He truly does, my friend. He changes people from the inside out—their lives, their circumstances, their perspectives. He will change you, too.

You can find the work of the Holy Spirit in each of the Bible's 66 books. The Book of Acts is sometimes called "The Acts of the Apostles." It is also referred to as "The Acts of the Holy Spirit," and that's the way I like to think of it. As you seek to go deeper in your walk with the Spirit of God, I would like to take you through this wonderful Book of Acts and show you, chapter by chapter, exactly what He can do in your life as you grow in your relationship with Him.

The Book of Acts is a record of the dramatic changes that happened in the lives of the apostles because of the fellowship of the Holy Spirit. When you welcome the Holy Spirit into your life, the same things can happen to you. As you read about the ways He can change you, pray to see these promises become a reality for you.

Acts 1: He'll change the way you hear.

Just before Jesus returned to heaven, He told His apostles not to leave Jerusalem, but to wait for "the Promise of the Father" that He had spoken to them about (Acts 1:4). He said, "For John truly baptized with water; but ye shall be baptized with the Holy Ghost not many days hence" (Acts 1:5).

The Lord's instructions were somewhat difficult for the apostles to understand. They knew well the fellowship of Jesus and how to enjoy a relationship with Him, but had no concept of what it meant to be baptized with the Spirit.

The Holy Spirit takes you beyond hearing with your ears and helps you listen with your heart. He gives you the understanding that comes from listening with your heart (spiritual hearing), in addition to the knowledge that comes from listening with your ears (physical hearing).

Acts 2: He'll change the way you speak.

When the Holy Spirit came upon the apostles, He changed their speech as they "began to speak with other tongues, as the Spirit gave them utterance" (Acts 2:4).

With the power he received at Pentecost, Peter declared the message of Christ, and three thousand people were added to the church in one day (see Acts 2:41).

Episcopalian Dennis Bennett, in his inspiring book, *The Holy Spirit and You*, explains it well: "He overflowed from them out into the world around, inspiring them to praise and glorify God, not only in their own tongues, but in the new languages, and in so doing, tamed their tongues to His use, freed their spirits, renewed their minds, refreshed their bodies, and brought power to witness."[15]

Acts 3: He'll change your appearance.

Here's what I notice about people with a strong anointing of the Holy Spirit on their lives. They look young, regardless of their age. Their eyes sparkle, and they have physical strength.

Years ago, I knew a minister whose countenance radiated with the presence of the Lord. I knew him for years and he had a great anointing of the Spirit upon his life and ministry. During his ministry, however, a major problem surfaced in his life. Instead of dealing with it, he chose to ignore it, and the presence of God left him. I saw him only a few months later and was shocked! He didn't even look like himself. He appeared to be a haggard old man. His zeal for life had vanished. He had aged years in just a few months. And even more tragic than the physical changes in his appearance, the anointing of the Holy Spirit no longer rested upon him as it once had.

After Peter and John were filled with the Holy Spirit, they went to the temple gate and a beggar asked them for money. The first words they spoke to him were, "Look on us" (Acts 3:4). You see, they knew that a look of power and boldness had come upon them because of God's presence. They knew that the life of the Holy Spirit on the inside of them had changed the way they looked on the outside and their whole countenance reflected an inner work of God's presence.

Instead of giving him money, Peter said, "Silver and gold have I none; but such as I have give I thee: In the name of Jesus Christ of Nazareth rise up and walk" (Acts 3:6).

The crippled beggar jumped to his feet and began running, leaping, and praising God. When the people saw what had occurred, "they were filled with wonder and amazement at that which had happened unto him" (Acts 3:10).

The presence of the Lord makes a difference in your life. The Holy Spirit even changes the way you look.

Acts 4: He'll change your behavior.

I have great difficulty whenever I try to fully describe what I experience during a service when the anointing of the Holy Spirit comes upon me. I become bold against satan and all his forces. I become a different man—fearless and without apprehension. Everything changes in a moment's time, all because of the wonderful anointing of the Holy Spirit.

I know from personal experience that the Holy Spirit truly does change an individual's behavior as the anointing of the Holy Spirit anoints a man or woman of God for service. On many occasions I have watched a video from a Miracle Crusade service or a television broadcast from a similar event. Each time I look on in total awe and wonder as I watch myself, the "Benny Hinn" on the television screen, minister with boldness and authority under the anointing of the Holy Spirit. I marvel at what I see myself do sometimes, for I know that it's the anointing of the Holy Spirit that makes the difference. It's an awesome experience, one that I treasure and thank the Lord for.

Because of the Holy Spirit, the behavior of Peter and John was drastically changed after the Day of Pentecost. Instead of fearing the Jews, they were proclaiming the message of the gospel with confidence. "Now when they saw the boldness of Peter and John, and perceived that they were unlearned and ignorant men, they marveled; and they took knowledge of them, that they had been with Jesus" (Acts 4:13). Isn't that beautiful? Because of the change in these men, people realized "that they had been with Jesus."

A relationship with the Holy Spirit gives you, among other gifts, three kinds of boldness: boldness to come before God, boldness with other people, and boldness against satan.

Who gave David the courage to do battle against Goliath? Who gave Paul the boldness to stand before King Agrippa and insist that Jesus is still alive? God's Holy Spirit.

He is still in the business of changing behavior.

Acts 5: He'll change your experience.

Peter had a new friend who may have been invisible to others but was a reality to him. He told the Sanhedrin, the supreme Jewish court, "We are his witnesses of these things; and *so is* also the Holy Ghost, whom God hath given to them that obey him" (Acts 5:32).

The disciples did not say, "We are His witnesses" or, "So are the soldiers who were there." The Holy Spirit was real to them, and the evidence of His presence in their lives was there for all to see. "God also bearing *them* witness, both with signs and wonders, and with divers miracles, and gifts of the Holy Ghost, according to his own will?" (Hebrews 2:4). They were actually seeing part of the power that Jesus had promised to them before He ascended into heaven (see Acts 1:8).

Oh, how wonderful it is to have the Holy Spirit as your Friend and Companion and to experience His reality each and every moment. He will never, ever leave you!

Acts 6: He'll change your position.

It is impossible to predict where your walk with the Holy Spirit will lead. The story of Stephen, as recorded in Acts, is a good example. He was not an apostle before becoming a deacon. Stephen was simply active in the church in Jerusalem, a man full of the Holy Spirit, and faith (see Acts 6:5).

It is apparent that the Holy Spirit was moving in a great and powerful way, touching not only the preachers but also the laymen, for the Bible says, "Stephen, full of faith and power, did great wonders and miracles among the people" (Acts 6:8).

How did he move from his position as a layman to a position in ministry as an usher or administrator, and then to an evangelist? He was moved because of his fellowship with the Holy Spirit. And because of this fellowship, the Holy Spirit gave him great authority and changed his position.

When members of the synagogue began to argue with Stephen, "they were not able to resist the wisdom and the spirit by which he spake" (Acts 6:10). He had a new position, and new authority in ministry. The beloved Holy Spirit can do the same for you.

Acts 7: He'll change your vision.

A relationship with the Holy Spirit will change what you see and how you see. Instead of looking down, you'll start looking up — where the horizon is much brighter. You'll see things differently than you do now, and you'll understand things you never have before.

Stephen was about to be bound and carried through the streets of Jerusalem and stoned for his faith, but the Holy Spirit gave him a glorious vision. The Bible says that he, "being full of the Holy Ghost, looked steadfastly into heaven, and saw the glory of God, and Jesus standing on the right hand of God" (Acts 7:55).

To get a new perspective, follow the advice of Paul in Colossians 3:2: "Set your affection on things above, not on things on the earth." This is the kind of vision God desires for His people to have, and the Holy Spirit is able to impart it to you.

Acts 8: He'll change your discernment.

Have you ever met a Christian who had no tact or wisdom when dealing with people who didn't know the Lord? I have, and I'll tell you, God is concerned with timing and with tact. He wants us to do things at the right time and in the right way.

When the perfect moment came to witness to an Ethiopian, "The Spirit said unto Philip, Go near, and join thyself to this chariot. And Philip ran . . ." (Acts 8:29-30).

Philip knew the voice of God so well that when the Spirit said, "Now," Philip responded instantly and ran. He didn't want to miss the opportunity.

During Paul's journeys, he did not witness to people until they were ready for it. Once, when he was on a ship headed for Rome, a violent storm erupted. If he had witnessed to the unbelievers when there was no temptest in their life, they probably would have turned a deaf ear. Paul had the right words. But more than that, he was sensitive to discern the right time. He spoke of "the angel of God, whose I am, and whom I serve, Saying, Fear not . . ." (Acts 27:23-24). He told them that God promised to protect all who sailed with him.

Don't trust your own judgment. Pray for the Holy Spirit to give you discernment; then follow His guidance. He will always lead you perfectly.

Acts 9: He'll change your attitude.

Saul, who later was called Paul, is a prime example of the way the Holy Spirit can transform your walk. Can you imagine calling someone who is a blasphemer, a persecutor, and a murderer, "Brother"?

To the natural ear, that sounds impossible. But that's what the Holy Spirit can do. He makes the impossible possible. When God told Ananias to go and pray for Saul, he argued: "Lord, I have heard by many of this man, how much evil he hath done to thy saints at Jerusalem:" (Acts 9:13).

Nevertheless, Ananias obeyed God and went to pray for Saul. The moment Ananias met him, he laid his hands on Saul and said, "Brother Saul, the Lord, *even* Jesus, that appeared unto thee in the way as thou camest, hath sent me, that thou mightest receive thy sight, and be filled with the Holy Ghost" (Acts 9:17).

Even the apostles didn't want to associate with Saul. They were not convinced of his conversion. As far as they knew, he had been on his way to Jerusalem to kill them, for they had seen no evidence to support that theory!

It took Barnabas to change their attitude. He brought Saul before them and explained "how he had seen the Lord in the way, and that he had spoken to him, and how he had preached boldly at Damascus in the name of Jesus" (Acts 9:27).

When the apostles saw the transformation that had taken place in Paul, they were amazed. He had turned one of the cruelest persecutors of the church into one of its champions. This man who had once been a threat to their own personal safety and to the message they preached now went about proclaiming "Christ in the synagogues, that he is the Son of God" (Acts 9:20).

If the Holy Spirit could transform Saul into Paul, totally re-orchestrating his life and the purpose for his very existence, imagine how He could transform you and me. Just one touch of His presence can change the course of our lives so that we will walk in His ways to accomplish His marvelous will and not our own.

Acts 10: He'll change your tradition.

My hometown of Jaffa, Israel, had the ancient Greek name of Joppa in Bible times. As a boy I climbed to the Citadel, a lighthouse on the highest spot overlooking the harbor. Near this lighthouse is the house of Simon the Tanner, where the apostle Peter had an experience that changed the world.

On the roof of Simon's house, Peter had a vision of God lowering four-footed animals, reptiles, and birds in a giant sheet. God told Peter to kill and eat them. Peter, a man bound by tradition, said, "Not so, Lord; for I have never eaten any thing that is common or unclean" (Acts 10:14).

The Lord answered, "What God hath cleansed, *that* call not thou common" (Acts 10:15).

While Peter thought about the vision, the Holy Spirit told him to go downstairs and meet three men who were looking for him. Furthermore, God said he should "go with them, doubting nothing: for I have sent them" (Acts 10:20).

Peter despised Gentiles. He was so bound by his Jewishness that, before this moment, he would not even talk to them. But because of the vision he had seen, Peter discarded his tradition and went on to have a great ministry to the Gentile world.

Only the Holy Spirit can produce such a radical transformation. What kind of transformation do you need? Ask Him to do it.

Acts 11: He'll change your outlook.

At times the Holy Spirit will reveal the future in preparation for trials and struggles coming your way. We find one instance of that in Acts 11:28: "And there stood up one of them named Agabus, and signified by the spirit that there should be great dearth throughout all the world: which came to pass in the day of Claudius Caesar."

When this kind of revelation occurs, there is no natural explanation for it. However, there is an inner knowing that what has been revealed to your heart will take place and that because of God's grace, He is preparing you for it. Through prayer you can be prepared for what is ahead. I challenge you this day to commit to a deeper, more intimate prayer life than you've ever known.

Acts 12: He'll change your prayer life.

It would have been totally impossible for me to develop a prayer life without first becoming acquainted with the Holy Spirit. It flows so naturally when you know Him, yet apart from Him it is impossible.

When the believers heard that Peter was in prison, "prayer was made without ceasing of the church unto God for him" (Acts 12:5). They learned what it meant to pray without ceasing.

This continual prayer was offered until the answer came for Peter and he was delivered from Herod's prison by an angel. The chains fell off and he walked out of the prison (see Acts 12:7).

In fact, God's divine intervention on Peter's behalf was so miraculous and out of the ordinary that Peter wasn't even sure it was actually happening. He thought he was having a vision. Just moments before his liberation, Peter had been sleeping, chained between two soldiers. Suddenly a bright light appeared in the prison, and an angel of the Lord woke him and said, "Arise up quickly" (Acts 12:7). And with that, Peter's chains fell off! Then the angel of the Lord told him to put his sandals on, wrap his garment around him, and follow him. Not until he was outside the prison, walking on the streets, did Peter realize what had really happened!

The believers in the Book of Acts were able to pray without ceasing for Peter because of the presence of the Holy Spirit, for prayer without ceasing is impossible without the help and assistance of the Holy Spirit. Ask Him today to develop that in you and He will. Psalm 80:18 declares, "Quicken us, and we will call upon thy name." Ask Him to quicken and revive you daily and He will do it.

Acts 13: He'll make your calling sure.

Since the moment the Holy Spirit called me to preach His Word, I have never had one moment of doubt concerning my calling. It was not an occupation chosen by trial and error, nor was it a decision I made for myself. God directed and I said yes.

Throughout the Book of Acts you will meet people who were called by God for a specific task. During a service at a church at Antioch, the Holy Spirit said, "Separate me Barnabas and Saul for the work whereunto I have called them" (Acts 13:2).

The church fasted, prayed, and laid their hands on them before sending the evangelists away. Scripture tells us they were "sent forth by the Holy Ghost" to the island of Cyprus (Acts 13:4).

There is only one way to know God's direction and leadership for your life. Continue to seek the Him until He makes your calling sure—and remember, the Holy Spirit speaks through the Scriptures and through godly people, as well as directly to your heart.

Acts 14: He'll change your authority.

As Paul and Barnabas ministered from city to city, there was a power in their preaching, an authority and confirmation to their words and deeds.

When they came to Lystra, a man who had never walked, heard them. And as Paul spoke, the man's faith came alive and Paul, "perceiving that he had faith to be healed, Said with a loud voice, 'Stand upright on thy feet'" (Acts 14:9-10). And the man—crippled from birth—leaped to his feet and began to walk.

Paul was watching the man while he preached, but waited to speak until the man was ready for his miracle. The Holy Spirit gave Paul that perception to know when the time for the miracle was right. Then, He gave Paul the authority to minister miraculously to that man. Allow the Holy Spirit to increase your authority, too.

Acts 15: He'll be your partner in decision-making.

I have discovered that one of the greatest benefits of walking with the Holy Spirit is that I don't have to make decisions alone. I have a Teacher, a Guide, and a Counselor to help me every step of the way. He is more than an advisor. He is deeply interested in everything that concerns you, and He wants to be a partner in settling every issue in your life.

When the church at Jerusalem sent a letter to the Gentile believers at Antioch, they wrote something of profound importance. They said, "It seemed good to the Holy Ghost, and to us" (Acts 15:28). They didn't make decisions on their own. These wise people knew to let the Holy Spirit help them.

The Spirit of God is a wonderful Companion, but He wants to become more than that to you. He knows the end from the beginning in everything you face. Allow Him to participate in your decision-making. You could not find a better Helper!

Acts 16: He'll change your direction.

More than once our staff has made detailed plans for a major crusade when the Holy Spirit has clearly warned me, "Don't go." I can't explain it and I certainly don't understand it, but I know how much He cares for me, and I have to obey His leading. When He speaks that way, we change our plans.

When Paul and Silas traveled through the region of Galatia, they "were forbidden of the Holy Ghost to preach the word in Asia, After they had come to Mysia, they assayed to go into Bithynia, but the Spirit suffered them not" (Acts 16:6-7).

That is when the Holy Spirit gave Paul a vision of a man from Macedonia, pleading, "Come over into Macedonia, and help us" (Acts 16:9).

You've heard this before, but it won't hurt to be reminded: "When God closes one door, He always opens another." It's true. Opening and closing doors is one way He clearly directs us.

When you let God chart your course, you will be on the right path. Remember, the Holy Spirit never makes a mistake. Trust Him to lead and He will do so with perfection.

Acts 17: He'll change your world.

At Thessalonica, Paul and Silas were involved in a near-riot, but it really wasn't their fault. The Jews were so jealous of the crowds who were listening to Paul explain the Scriptures that they rounded up some unsavory characters at the marketplace, formed a mob, and started a riot in the city (see Acts 17:1-5).

The throng shouted to the rulers of the city, "These that have turned the world upside down are come hither also" (Acts 17:6).

Their reputation preceded Paul and Silas, and news of their activities spread quickly. Almost everywhere they went, they saw a revival. People were turning to Christ, healings were taking place; and the Spirit of God was at work.

And He wants to do the same through you today. He really wants to change your world.

Years ago, someone told me, "Benny, the quickest way to turn your world upside down is to turn yourself right-side up." It was good advice.

Acts 18: He'll change your understanding.

You will begin to know the ways of God more perfectly. You will find that you now understand truths or things in God's Word that were once baffling to you. I feel fortunate to be surrounded in ministry by people who have a deep dedication to the task God has called them to do. I am grateful for the sensitivity and understanding with which they minister as they serve Him. They have developed such sensitivity and understanding as a result of their relationship with the Holy Spirit.

"And he began to speak boldly in the synagogue: whom when Aquila and Priscilla heard, they took him unto *them*, and expounded unto him the way of God more perfectly" (Acts 18:26).

Acts 19: He'll change others as His presence comes upon you.

When Paul came to Ephesus, he found some disciples and said to them, "Have ye received the Holy Ghost since ye believed?" The disciples to whom he spoke answered, "We have not so much as heard whether there be any Holy Ghost." (Acts 19:2).

We find that Paul taught them about the Holy Spirit and then laid hands upon them, and "the Holy Ghost came on them" (Acts 19:6).

Later in this same chapter, we find that "God wrought special miracles by the hands of Paul: So that even from his body were brought unto the sick handkerchiefs or aprons, and the diseases departed from them, and the evil spirits went out of them" (Acts 19:11-12). The presence of God was so strong on Paul that the anointing could be transferred by the laying on of hands and upon handkerchiefs. The sick were healed and evil spirits were cast out because the anointing of the Holy Spirit lingered so powerfully upon Paul.

Paul was greatly opposed in Ephesus by both the Jewish establishment and the followers of pagan religions (see Acts 19:9, 23-41). Never forget that the greater the opposition, the greater the power. In this difficult and dangerous city, "God wrought special [literally, "extraordinary"] miracles" (Acts 19:11). The Holy Spirit wants to do the same today, only if we are willing to pay the price, which means being totally, completely, wholly yielded to Him.

Acts 20: He'll change your leadership.

God did not send His Spirit to earth as our Helper so that we could neglect our duties. As a Counselor and Guide, He shows us how to take responsibility for God's work and empowers us to do it with supernatural results, giving us a place of responsibility and influence in the Kingdom.

Paul's farewell message to the Ephesian elders after three years of ministry came straight from his heart. His objective was for them to accept the mantle of leadership in the church. He told them with great emotion, "Take heed therefore unto yourselves, and to all the flock, over the which the Holy Ghost hath made you overseers, to feed the church of God, which he hath purchased with his own blood" (Acts 20:28).

Paul issued this challenge with great confidence because he knew the Holy Spirit would give them all they needed to succeed, in spiritual leadership. He also knew that after his departure, "grievous wolves [will] enter in among you, not sparing the flock" (Acts 20:29). They would be determined to distort the truth and deceive the disciples.

God took Moses, who "*was* very meek, above all the men which *were* upon the face of the earth" (Numbers 12:3), and made him into a great leader. And He wants to do the same for you and through you today.

Acts 21: He'll change your insight.

At times God has given me a specific word of prophecy for someone. Sometimes this will happen as an individual stands before me on the platform in the crusades. So far, however, the Lord has never asked of me what he asked of Agabus. When He gave Agabus a word from God for Paul — the Billy Graham of his day — he did not shrink from delivering it. At Caesarea, Agabus walked up to the apostle, took Paul's belt, and bound it around his own hands and feet. Then he said, "Thus saith the Holy Ghost, 'So shall the Jews at Jerusalem bind the man that owneth this girdle, and shall deliver *him* into the hands of the Gentiles'" (Acts 21:11).

Only a man who had a mighty relationship with the Lord could make such a declaration.

Agabus' prophecy gave Paul insight into the difficult days ahead for him. He responded, "What mean ye to weep and to break mine heart? for I am ready not to be bound only, but also to die at Jerusalem for the name of the Lord Jesus" (Acts 21:13).

When we receive insight, it makes us bold and loyal, even unto death. When you know the Holy Spirit, you will see beyond the temporal, and not even death will frighten you.

Acts 22: He'll change your commission.

Do you remember the moment you gave your heart to Christ? Paul's experience on the Damascus road was one he certainly could not forget. Like so many people, Paul was sincere — but sincerely wrong. Paul had no use for Jesus or His followers. Although he took his opposition of Christ to an extreme, he was not unlike many of us in the days before we met the Master.

And meet the Master he did! Paul gave his testimony of being blinded by a bright light, and how his night turned to day. He had seen the resurrected Christ, and that convinced him of the truth of the gospel. From a changed recognition came a changed commission. "The God of our fathers hath chosen thee, that thou shouldest know his will, and see that Just One, and shouldest hear the voice of his mouth. For thou shalt be his witness unto all men of what thou hast seen and heard" (Acts 22:14-15).

Acts 23: He'll increase your influence.

People continue to ask, "Does the Lord really speak to people?" My answer is an unqualified yes! I know this not only because of my personal experience, but because God's Word says it's true!

The city of Jerusalem was in such an uproar over Paul that the commander of the prison thought the mobs would take him away by force. In the midst of that crisis, Scripture says, "The Lord stood by him, and said, 'Be of good cheer, Paul: for as thou hast testified of me in Jerusalem, so must thou bear witness also at Rome'" (Acts 23:11).

Because of God's power on his life, Paul was brought before Caesar and testified for the Master. And as Paul remained faithful, God opened doors supernaturally for him and brought him into a greater dimension of influence before men of power and authority for the glory of God. He became, and is to this day, a hero of our faith.

Acts 24: He'll establish your eternal hope.

The Apostle Paul was on a mission. No matter what his circumstances were, he presented the gospel. And Paul was supernaturally aided to do what he did and nothing could shake his commitment.

As Paul stood accused before the governor, he said, "But this I confess unto thee, that after the way which they call heresy, so I worship the God of my fathers, believing all things which are written in the law and in the prophets: And have hope toward God, which they themselves also allow, that there shall be a resurrection of the dead, both of the just and the unjust" (Acts 24:14-15). Here Paul declares that he was given hope—the marvelous hope given only by the Holy Spirit, even in the presence of his enemies.

Acts 25: He'll change your level of confidence.

Paul's reliance on the Lord never wavered. In the face of the Jews who hated him and the Romans who were baffled by him, he remained not only confident, but lively and aggressive!

He boldly maintained that "to the Jews have I done no wrong, as thou very well knowest . . . I appeal unto Caesar" (Acts 25:10-11). Now make no mistake, the Romans had heard Paul's message—even though they didn't quite understand it yet. In fact, the Roman official noted his understanding that Paul's message was about "Jesus, which was dead, whom Paul affirmed to be alive" (Acts 25:19). What baffled them was that Paul not only affirmed it, he was totally convinced of it.

How did Paul know Christ was alive in the loneliness of a prison cell, in the pain of a flogging, or in the desolation of a shipwreck? Through his never-ending companionship with the Holy Spirit he knew. The Lord Jesus not only promised to send the Comforter, but He delivered on that commitment. The Holy Spirit will be with you, too, in all the tough times you encounter.

Acts 26: He'll change your witness.

Before God healed my stuttering tongue, I would avoid speaking if at all possible. Even as a young Christian, I would never volunteer to read the Scripture in public or give even a short testimony.

But what a change took place when God healed me as I preached my first sermon in late 1974. My tongue was loosed, and it seems I have not stopped talking since.

Paul took every opportunity to present his testimony, too, and to bring deliverance to the captives. His defense before King Agrippa was so strong it has been a model of study for legal scholars. There was strength in his witness and power in his words. When he was finished, Agrippa said, "Almost thou persuadest me to be a Christian" (Acts 26:28).

Almost anyone can produce a speech, but only the Spirit of God can produce a testimony.

Acts 27: He'll change your chaos into peace.

On his final journey to Rome, Paul was a prisoner on a ship with 276 passengers. After two weeks of storm-tossed seas, the apostle was the only person who knew the meaning of peace. As day was about to dawn, "Paul besought *them* all to take meat, saying, 'This day is the fourteenth day that ye have tarried and continued fasting, having taken nothing'" (Acts 27:33).

He not only urged them to eat for survival, but reassured them, "there shall not an hair fall from the head of any of you" (Acts 27:34). In times of testing, only the peace from above can calm the storm.

I know what it is like to be near the point of death. In 1983, while flying with six passengers in a Cessna aircraft at 11,000 feet, we ran out of fuel near Avon Park, Florida. I was asleep, but not for long. "We're in trouble. Pray! Pray!" were the first words I heard from our pilot, Don.

Everyone began crying out in fear. But suddenly a great peace came over me. I said, "Don, it's going to be all right. No one will be killed!"

God used those words to calm the passengers. "Please don't cry," I told them. "Just relax. God isn't finished with me."

We crash-landed in a field and there were some injuries, but I did not have a scratch. Deep within my spirit I had the assurance, "It's going to be all right."

Over twenty years later, I faced similar circumstances in 1995. We were returning from a miracle crusade in Japan, heading for Hawaii where we were to land and refuel. With less than two hours left in our flight, silence in the cabin was interrupted by the pilot's voice as he said, "Pastor Benny, I think you'd better pray." He went on to explain that there was a problem with the instruments and we were lost somewhere over the Pacific.

I immediately began to pray and even though some of those who were with me were fearful, a peace settled over me. Although the circumstances were impossible in the natural, I felt a supernatural assurance that everything was going to be all right.

The pilots continued to work with the instruments in the cockpit, but to no avail. With a rapidly diminishing fuel supply and in the midst of growing tension, the unexplainable confidence within me continued — everything was going to be fine.

Suddenly and miraculously, our pilots made contact with someone who suggested that they tune to a radio station and use it to help guide them toward land. They did just that and landed with less than an hour's fuel remaining. In fact, our pilots told us we were flying on fumes!

Although I always knew that our safe landing was a direct result of God's divine intervention, I never knew any of the details. Just recently at our Hawaii Miracle Crusade, however, I had the privilege of meeting one of the gentlemen who was working in the control tower that night. He explained that although he wasn't responsible for that particular airspace, he felt an urging by the Holy Spirit to get involved when he heard one of the other controllers attempting to contact a private plane that was overdue. He said landings are scheduled in advance, and the control tower was expecting our plane. However, because the plane was off course due to the instrumentation problem, we never showed up on their radar. As they attempted to contact us, they finally made radio contact with the plane, but had no idea of our location.

As the man became more involved, he felt an overwhelming inner urging to pray. He explained, "I didn't know who was on that plane, but I knew that I had to help. When nothing else worked, someone in the tower suggested tuning into a radio station to help guide the plane in," the gentleman said. "I instantly remembered a 50,000-watt Christian radio station on the island which I listened to often. I suggested that frequency, and immediately, your pilots tuned in to the signal. That's how my friend and I in the control tower helped get your plane down on the ground safely."

Then he added, "For seven years I have wondered who was on that airplane that night but had no way of finding out. Recently, I was talking to some friends at our church about the situation and they told me they knew the other part of the story. They said they were Covenant Partners with Benny Hinn Ministries, and Benny Hinn and some of his team were the individuals on that plane that night."

After the man finished his story, I gave him a big hug and thanked him for recognizing the voice of the Holy Spirit and for responding in obedience. Then I added, "Thank you for saving my life! God wasn't done with me yet!"

I have seen the Holy Spirit turn chaos into peace many, many times. And I am a living testimony to His ability to do so. Won't you allow Him to touch the chaos in your life with His deep and abiding peace?

Acts 28: He'll change your conflict into victory.

Paul was shipwrecked off the island of Malta, and every passenger reached land in safety. But as they were building a fire for warmth, a viper came out of the heat and fastened itself on to Paul's hand.

When the island natives saw the snake hanging from his hand, they said to each other, "No doubt this man is a murderer, whom, though he hath escaped the sea, yet vengeance suffereth not to live" (Acts 28:4).

Instead of screaming, "I'm going to die! Get me some medicine!" Paul simply shook the serpent off and sustained no ill effects.

The islanders expected him to die instantly. After a while, when they realized he was going to live, "they changed their minds, and said that he was a god" (Acts 28:6).

Only the Holy Spirit can turn your conflict into victory. He'll do it for you!s

In Conclusion

The great message of the Book of Acts is this: Nothing can replace a personal relationship with the Holy Spirit. He works so mightily in the lives of people attuned to Him. The Upper Room experience is wonderful, but it's only the first step on a road of ever-increasing fellowship.

You need to know the Holy Spirit intimately, and He longs to fellowship with you. Allow Him now to change your hearing, your speech, your vision, your actions, and every part of your being. Start now to practice His presence, and to let Him change your life. Seek to know Him with your whole heart and fellowship with Him. As you do, the glory of His presence will touch your life, and help you go deeper with the wonderful Holy Spirit. When this happens, you will never be the same!

Endnotes

1. Lewis Sperry Chafer, *Systematic Theology*, Vol. 7 (Dallas, TX: Dallas Seminary Press, 1948), p. 188.

2. John F. Walvoord, *The Doctrine of the Holy Spirit*, as quoted in Chafer, Vol. 7, p. 20.

3. *Discipleship Journal* #36, p. 11.

4. Ibid, p. 7.

5. Joseph Bayly, *Decision Magazine*, May 1978.

6. Laird Harris, Gleason L. Archer and Bruce K. Waltke, *Theological Wordbook of the Old Testament* (Chicago: Moody, 1980), Vol. 1, p. 304.

7. Ibid, p. 103.

8. *The Autobiography of Bertrand Russell* (Little and Brown, 1967).

9. John F. Walvoord and Roy B. Zuck, eds., *Bible Knowledge Commentary, Old Testament* (Wheaton, IL: Victor Books, 1985) p. 1056.

10. Don Meredith, *Who Says Get Married* (Nashville, TN: Thomas Nelson), p. 42.

11. *Single Adult Ministries Newsletter*, Vol. 17, No. 5, March 1990, p. 1.

12. Robert Hanna, *A Grammatical Aid to the Greek New Testament* (Grand Rapids: Baker, 1983), p. 348.

13. Ibid, p. 176.

14. Chafer, Vol. 7, p. 23.

15.   Dennis Bennett, *The Holy Spirit and You* (Plainfield, NJ: Logos International, 1971), p. 28.

Benny Hinn has a mandate from God to take the message of God's saving and healing power across America and around the world through miracle crusades and television. To learn how to become a Covenant Partner In Ministry with Benny Hinn, call 817-722-2222 or simply write to:

Benny Hinn Ministries
P. O. Box 162000
Irving, TX 75016-2000